Christoph Noe

Swapping Arty VIP Pass for Happy Meal

Verlag für moderne Kunst

Dedicated to the art people who see being kind not as a strategy but as a way of life.

If not in the art world, then where else can we dream?

Welcome to the sequel of *How To Not Fuck Up Your Art-World Happiness*. For those who have read the first volume, it seems you have answered the last piece of advice—"#60 Accept throwing in the towel"—with a "no," a "not yet," or maybe with a "never ever" since you are still here, working, living, breathing (or at least interested) in the art world. For those new to the series, this is as good of a place as any to join the conversation (definitely not small talk—see "#2 Go beyond the small talk") on happiness in the art world.

Obviously, I am also still part of the art circus despite full happiness having not yet arrived within the last two years since the first book was published. Maybe even the opposite is true; my confusion has risen. A heightened sense of fragility within the art market; the emergence of absurd "allow lists" naming those worthy enough to receive permission to purchase artworks; artists and many art workers struggling for acknowledgement and financial success; NFTs, fractionalization, Balenciaga boots, and Metaverse and Co. being hyped. My problem does not have to do with innovation at all. Rather, my concern lies in the fact that many of the "innovations" being created are not making our world in any way more exciting, human, or livable but only serve the purpose of making sales and generating profits.

Suffice to say, my love-hate relationship with the art world has intensified. I find myself simultaneously fascinated, excited, and believing it is something too precious to let go, while on many days also feeling full of despair and coming to the conclusion that the art world is just a corporate, transactional place without any magic to it. That said, I am the first to admit the art world is not the worst place to be in, and things could be worse. Nonetheless, here we are discussing how things can be better.

Compared to the first publication, this book is in some parts even more honest, more unfiltered, more personal, and more serious. Some of the advice and tips might even sound more simple, more obvious, and more general. But as we know so well, the most simple and obvious things are often the most difficult ones to hold on to. In conversations with friends working in industries outside the art world, I start to wonder if the topics discussed here are broad enough that they could be equally applied to other fields. Not all the advice given is fully new, but it elaborates on topics that have been addressed in different forms before. If you notice that some thoughts are slightly contradictory, I won't argue against it. The (art) world is paradox, things are changing, and often issues are not as clear as they might seem. As such, I have come to terms with being confused. You may want to allow this for yourself too. We have seen great things coming out of confusion, after all. Another key theme in this volume is advice not only on how to create happiness for yourself but also for others. What goes around comes around, and you will ultimately benefit from your generosity. Lastly, as you might have figured out already, this book cannot provide ultimate happiness. Instead, it becomes a playground on which questions and answers can grow.

It is flattering and simultaneously worrying (worrying because happiness, or the lack thereof, seems to be a major issue in the art world) having received such overwhelming feedback on the first publication. For me, the most positive and encouraging message is that other people are resonating with the topic of happiness in the art world, and that we are not alone, pushing together for change for good. Please be constantly reminded that your/our actions, no matter how small you think they are, can make a difference (see “#9 Be a motivator”).

So, what is my take in 2024? Working or being part of the art world is a continuous challenge that needs (self-)reflection, action, belief, trust, endurance, and a good sense of humor to survive. This book continues to look at the art world in this way, a place many of us inhabit in our professions and daily lives and call “home.”

Once again, I want to thank my colleagues, allies, friends, and art world crew for being with me on this rollercoaster, making it fully worth the ride. Of course, I want to thank my wonderful editor, graphic designer, and publisher for their parts in realizing such a publication once again. My thanks go also to everyone who gave me input for new tips and hacks. In the tradition of a storyteller, I often feel as merely a recorder and documenter of things that happen around me. When I write as “I” or “me,” it is often “we” who I am really referring to.

Christoph Noe
Somewhere in the art world, August 2024

TABLE OF CONTENTS

SE-
LECT Ø1
YOUR
WORK
FAMILY
WISE-
LY

Miami Beach, champagne receptions, business (possibly replaced by economy these days) flights around the world, spine-tingling art experiences, sharing tears and moments of joy. Sounds like life with your girlfriend/boyfriend/partner? Nope. We are talking about your work-wife or work-husband. Let's do some easy math: You work from the age of 28 (assuming two master's degrees and some more education at an arts education institute, etc.) until the age of 75 (and here already anticipating an increased retirement age). During those 40–50 working years, you change your job every two to 10 years. If we now assume a marriage lasts only … you understand what I want to say. A number of couples spend much less time with each other than with their work partners. So when choosing a new job, your new colleagues should be a crucial factor to consider.

GO BEYOND THE SMALL TALK

02

There are situations when small talk cannot be avoided. That's accepted. But at least never waste your time. Here are my top six questions to spice up any small talk situation and turn it into a real conversation:

1. Would you rather buy a good artwork by a bad artist or a bad artwork by a good artist?

2. Is an artwork painted with UV color that glows at night more valuable on the secondary market than one with no UV color? (An actual question that I was asked.)

3. Is it ever okay to dispose of an artwork? (Asking for a friend. The storage costs have already surpassed the value of the work by more than ten times.)

4. Are art people around non-art people more lost than the other way around?

5. Would people go to art exhibitions if they were as expensive as concert tickets?

6. Is it acceptable to present a Mike Kelley Christmas tree buttplug on Christmas Eve to your non-art family members?

03

EM-BRACE THE EL-DERLY

Aging is inevitable. At some point, you will find that when you go to a party (of course, not an art party) you are more often the shuttle for your kids than partying yourself. However, that should not make you age out of relevancy. We have seen a number of those “40 Under 40” lists (the author, too, has contributed to the creation of such lists) but where are the stories about the senior citizens? It would be refreshing to hear about a seventy-eight-year-old joining a blue-chip gallery straight from the old people’s home or a retired fireman turning into a museum tour guide or perhaps an editor that conceived art museum guides for senior peers. Let’s explore the other side of the age spectrum; otherwise, the pursuit of youth may result in a “10 Nepo-Kids Under 10” list.

When times and business are not easy, relationships are often dropped quicker than Lee Ufan drops a stone on a glass plate. A typical scenario in a gallery-artist relationship: When one show is not fully sold, it's ciao ciao to the artist to whom the gallery had been sending Instagram DMs from dawn to midnight, wooing them to paint 25 canvases in five weeks for a solo show. While the tale of Vincent and his brother Theo, who managed to sell only one of his paintings during Vincent's lifetime yet maintained unwavering faith, may sound a tad too romantic, it still resonates. There are people operating like lone wolves in the world as never before. People don't want to compromise. They want it all. And now. In good times as in bad times, with all the economic pressures understood, creating a relationship for business and life can take some time and pain. Let's not always be out only for ourselves and instead show some more loyalty. Ultimately, loyalty can yield significant rewards.

04

STICK TOGETH-ER—IN GOOD TIMES AND IN BAD

SELL ART-WORKS ON DAT-ING APPS

Ø5

Recently, an artist told me she is selling artworks via Raya. How so? She wrote in her bio, "Not interested in dating but in selling artworks." And it works. She has already made a number of sales. Maybe it's unsurprising since the press has already named LinkedIn the new Raya, but could Raya or Hinge be the new Artsy? Perhaps not so, but it does demonstrate that a creative usage of such a platform can amplify an artist's reach and provide access to new audiences. Is this how our traditional art system expects us to work? Probably not. Should we care? Most likely not. Is this approach for everyone? Definitely not. But in her case, it's effective. She is autonomous and she is successful. How can cheekiness and out-of-the-art-box concepts help you?

DON'T 06 WASTE

I frequently encounter individuals stuck in dissatisfaction with their current jobs or positions, contemplating a change for years. However, despite the desire for transformation, passivity sets in, and complaints persist unchanged over time. The longer one remains in an unhappy situation, the more it becomes the accepted norm. Simultaneously, the perceived risks of change escalate, especially as life progresses with added responsibilities like family support, larger homes, more expensive lifestyles, the request to have a certain title on the business card, etc. The stakes associated with change

TIME

and reinventing oneself become higher. Therefore, do it now. You know what is later? Later, your coffee gets cold. Later, the opportunity is gone. Later, part of your life is over. So how to do it? If it is challenging to incorporate big changes, start with small changes and habits. A dual strategy might be the most pragmatic approach, meaning you don't have to resign immediately from everything you do now; first steps can go in parallel. Start working on something new after work or hustling alongside your regular 9-to-5. The time for change is now.

DETOX

DIGI-TALLY

07

Let me play the Marie Kondo of the arts here. The minimalist suggests putting all things you are not sure about in boxes and moving them down to your basement. After three months, assess whether you miss them. If not, dispose of them. What does that mean for the digital cleaning side? Delete old files of 100 MB auction catalogue pdfs, unsubscribe from those dozen newsletters that distract your attention, remove timewasting art apps. The list could go on. Don't forget to apply the same principle to Instagram. Unfollow the account and save the username in a separate file. After a few months, reassess. If the absence goes unnoticed, it is time to empty your digital trash bin.

The art world has so many functions:

- education provider
- hedge fund
- dating portal
- think tank
- rich tweens day- (and night-) care
- amusement park
- soft power source
- political and social opinion generator
- therapy
- wall decoration
- competition venue
- social glue

And there are many more. Don't try to put art mentally into one box only. Its beauty lies in its ability to offer diverse meanings to different individuals. Embrace its various facets and discover the joy and value they bring to your life.

ENJOY THE MULTI-PLE FUNC-TIONS 08 OF THE ART WORLD

Ø9

BE A MOTI-VATOR

A few years ago, I encountered a young aspiring interior designer. With her limited English and my limited Italian at the time, our conversation wasn't entirely fluent. Despite this, a warm connection formed, and we both expressed genuine interest and appreciation for each other's work. We have stayed connected over the years, and recently, her projects were featured in the Italian edition of *Architectural Digest*. Witnessing her achievements has been truly exciting. She shared that our meeting years ago held significance for her: It motivated her to improve her English proficiency, enabling her to present her projects internationally, while also serving as a source of encouragement during a time when international design media showed limited interest in her work. Her success is undoubtedly a result of her hard work, yet the realization that a simple coffee meeting on a Tuesday afternoon played a part in motivating her underscores the impact such connections can have.

Overheard: At a recent auction preview, I found myself in front of a painting by the artist Jason Boyd Kinsella. An art advisor from the auction house passed by with a client and, to my surprise, mistakenly introduced the artwork as a creation by George Condo. Although, and especially when scrolling at a speed of five Instagram posts per second, both artists exhibit an eclectic style often painting distorted figures, they are not the same. Of course, it is impossible to have a full overview of all artists, and errors are inherent to human nature. However, in a professional role, maintaining a high (I am too disillusioned to use the word "highest") professional standard is imperative. This means thorough research, diligent homework, and a focus on talking about what one knows with certainty (many art exhibition openings would be very quiet then, I assume). After all, winning is often being the person in the room with the most (insider) information. Professionalism is not only beneficial for personal credibility but also for the wider community of art colleagues.

KNOW

WHAT YOU ARE TALK-ING ABOUT

1Ø

11

USE THE ART DEALER CHECKLIST

Some complaints we continuously notice relate to requests for secondary market works. I previously addressed this issue by recommending the importance of keeping the art-dealer chain short and straightforward. The next question that arises is how to determine the length of the dealer chain. For a practical solution, ask the following questions: What series of the artist is the client looking for? What size? Which material? What is the budget? Has the client bid at auction for the artist before, and if yes, on which work? You would be surprised how often the inquirer (aka a seasoned art dealer) is unable to answer such questions swiftly. If so, this is a clear indication that the homework has not been done to understand precisely the client's request, and, more often than not, they are not directly working with the client but playing the telephone game. Hands off!

Art world parents listen: Don't force your kids to share your love for art. It can be wonderful to share it with a close person and have conversations about things you love together. However, art is often very personal and collecting even more so. We have seen major collectors sell their collections and close their museums after discussions with their children about whether they want to take over or not. I think that is a fair decision to accept for the outside world. No hard feelings. The collection was a personal journey as is departing from it. Anyway, how can we be sure that our Bearbrick toy figurine collection doesn't look to our kids like what our grandma's doll collection looked like to us?

LET YOUR KIDS LIVE OUT-SIDE THE ART WORLD

12

Undoubtedly there is magic in art: Creating something that cannot be expressed in words, only artworks can do. Having been in the industry for an extended period now, it has occurred to me that some of this "magic" is very obvious and purely crowd-pleasing. Examples: The artwork is super big, the artwork is super small, the artwork is at a location you don't expect or the location itself is a surprise. Popular artistic concepts are also multiplying endlessly, be it infinity mirrors in some new shape or form, or huge digital animations that would look just like a psychedelic screensaver on your old Windows PC if it weren't for the music.
I do like to stand in front of works with eyes open, captivated by the story and visuals. Unfortunately, simple and often noisy concepts tend to overshadow quieter and more sensitive concepts. Continue to be critical and to look for the less loud and obvious artistic proposals.

DON'T BE TRICKED 13

14 INVEST IN EDUCATION

I am discussing this with a particular agenda: We have consistently advocated for collaboration with art institutions and academia. Indeed, investing in education can be immensely valuable, particularly during periods of lower activity such as when between jobs, offering opportunities for new impulses and ideas. However, it's not only the educational content that holds significance; the network you gain access to is crucial. Therefore, when selecting an education provider, pay close attention to the alumni program they offer. Access to a strong network is equally decisive.

QUES-TION LIST-INGS 15

Rankings and top lists are a double-edged sword. Trust me, I know this very well having created a number of them. The names on it love you while the ones off it don't. And the ones trying to be on it do everything they can to be in the next edition. I remember being followed not just into the bathroom but up to the pissoir by a collector chatting me up while we both … used the facilities, questioning his non-listing. For the (self-proclaimed) KOLs, influencers, and VIPs, such titles often imply that their opinions and words are the truth and carry significant weight, resulting in a sense of entitlement that may or may not be deserved.

Are these rankings and titles up for discussion? Certainly. Even those based on hard numbers are not without flaws: The most visited art fairs might just mean that the queues at the entrance are longer, the blockbuster show that the ticket prices are higher, the rising art star that they have more likes on Instagram. Listings and labels are often strategies employed by the media, museums, galleries, and other players in the industry who carry strong agendas sometimes also influenced by corporates and brands.
So why are we still publishing listings? We want to acknowledge certain contributions and achievements, but please question the source and context. I invite you to be fully critical of them as much as of any influencer's "hot buy" recommendation.

Watch guru Jean-Claude Biver said it best: "As a successful person, you don't have any privileges. Just because you received a Ph.D. or carry a famous name does not mean that you are automatically treated special. Only a few have received the biggest privilege of being successful." Rather, there is an implied duty to share and a sense of not only "noblesse oblige" but also "success oblige." I am afraid that the people who should read this are not always part of the audience. They will continue to run over everyone and everything that comes in their way to a VIP fair preview, knocking your 25 Swiss francs raclette pfännchen out of your hand on a hot June day.

And speaking of fairs, the security staff are just doing their job. Don't be grumpy and open your damn Loewe bag (in which a small painting could easily fit).

*Jean-Claude Biver: *Du kannst alles, wenn Du nur willst*

16 DON'T ABUSE PRIVI-LEGES

DO

17

NOTH-
ING

It feels like one of the hardest things to achieve. We are consistently in a state of "doing," and even in our moments of relaxation we find ourselves still engaged in multiple activities: from yoga to exploring consciousness and meditating to scrolling on screens and traveling the art world to another city to see art we just saw. On top of that, external pressures such as selling works, making works, and collecting works persist, and all alongside managing daily life and economic concerns. You add to the list. Harald Juhnke (for all non-Germans and young readers, he was a famous German entertainer) once defined happiness with the phrase, "No appointments and being a bit tipsy." Please note that he was an alcoholic and that the author does not encourage any use of drugs. Nonetheless, I firmly believe that it shouldn't be considered a luxury but rather a natural part of our routine to engage in activities that involve doing nothing or undertaking monotonous tasks, allowing our minds to wander. This unstructured time is crucial for the brain to function and generate innovative ideas. Creative concepts need space to grow.

Side note: This tip came to the author on a sunny early December afternoon walking the dog, not actively thinking about anything.

A number of studies on the future of employment have come to the same conclusion: Professions in the arts sector have one of the strongest growth potentials over the next few years, unlike jobs such as drivers and accountants. In other words, most of our jobs are highly unlikely to be automatized. Isn't that great news? For some, this might bear only a little comfort as you struggle along as a young gallerist or emerging artist. It will also depend on how much flexibility you show, sticking only to traditional routes or being open to unleashing your artistic potential in other ways. I don't believe that an artwork can be the only artistic output. In my opinion, artists will be required more than ever to tell us stories, to help us dream, to solve problems, to support society, the economy, politics, and companies seeking to look at problems in different ways, to teach kids and adults alike how to use the left brain, and how to creatively work with grief, loss, and other big emotions. So, no matter the final output, be assured that you are generally in the right scene.

BE FU-TURE-PROOF

18

SUR-PRISE YOUR-SELF

19

Breaking patterns can be quite challenging. I am talking about the years in and out of traveling to the same fairs annually, visiting the same galleries for every opening, checking the same news webpages daily, and scrolling the same friends' feeds on IG hourly. Do you also get the feeling that this is just like flipping through a *Vogue* or *Men's Health* magazine? You don't know if it is from 2018 or last week (except that fats and carbs cycle annually between lethal and wonder weapons). A routine can make time fly by, and we might even lose track of what we did when. Here's a proposal: Embrace change, replace the familiar with something new, and try unexplored activities. Venture into that small gallery down the street you always passed but never entered. Borrow a pottery wheel from a friend and craft your own muesli bowl (intentionally avoiding the mention of an ashtray). Pick up a conversation with a gallerist, and don't be shy to ask about prices. Take the bold step of giving a friend, a client, etc. an unannounced video call. Visit a non-art museum. Step off your home turf, break free from your comfort zone, and disrupt your routine!

This book also serves as a personal call to action. I recognize that expressing gratitude is an area where I can enhance my own behavior, as I find myself becoming frustrated when others don't reciprocate. Whether it's requesting price lists from artists, inquiring about transportation quotes, or checking the opening times of private museums, people (myself included) reach out for information. On the receiving end, there are people who invest time and effort to address these inquiries seriously.
Once a reply is received, it's a matter of courtesy to express thanks or acknowledgment. It appears to be a phenomenon of our time where there is a readiness to request things when needed but a lack of emphasis on expressing gratitude when the request is fulfilled. Implementing this simple practice can instantly bring more happiness to others and, ultimately, what goes around comes around.

20 HIT THE REPLY BUTTON

The genuinely motivational account @inspired-towrite recently touched upon this, emphasizing the importance of reassuring artists and creatives that their identity as an artist persists regardless of their current level of productivity. The account aptly states, "Time away from art is never time away from being an artist. It is not wasting time; it is often gathering material and collecting experiences that will be injected into future creations. You are not a bad artist when you are not creating right now." Creative ideas need space and cannot always be forced. The same logic applies to artists who have not sold a work in 2024 yet. You are valid.

21 KNOW YOUR VAL-UE

22 PICK UP THE PHONE

Only idiots think they can win an argument in a text thread. As I was reflecting on this comment I came across recently, I realized that I've fallen into this trap multiple times (and still do). The written word is on paper/on pdf/saved in the chat history, and therefore set in stone. I can recall instances where email exchanges, initially centered around innocuous topics, spiraled into heated disputes, each reply intensifying the hostility and hindering a constructive resolution. A seemingly harmless conversation turned into a critical situation due to a misplaced word or a misinterpreted comma. Verbal communication, on the other hand, offers greater flexibility to gauge reactions, decipher nuances, and perceive the emotions of the other party. Hence, I would like to put forth a bold suggestion, particularly to millennial readers: Summon the courage to initiate a call and attempt to resolve the issue directly. Although it may require overcoming initial hesitation, it could prove to be more successful in the end.

23

DON'T DO EVERYTHING FOR FREE, BUT ALSO DON'T CHARGE FOR EVERYTHING

I've previously emphasized the importance of not working for free, a stance I remain steadfast in. However, this advice has stirred strong reactions and sparked conversations within our audience. In light of this, I want to add another layer to the discussion. It's crucial not to approach every interaction with a mentality of keeping a stopwatch to later charge for your efforts. While fair payment is essential, there are instances where providing assistance for free is not only acceptable but commendable. This includes helping friends, especially during times of crisis, and when you intuitively sense it's the right thing to do. Karma points: Giving something without the expectation of receiving something in return.

Dealing with administration and processes can be painful, and one of the luxuries I appreciate in my chosen career path is not having to engage in administrative and reporting tasks just for the sake of it. This is particularly true when it comes to serving middle management, which defines itself by the relevance of requesting reports, aggregating information, and redistributing it. In my opinion, it wouldn't be a tragedy if this were a thing of the past. But let's get back to the main topic. While I advocate for minimizing unnecessary bureaucracy, I still strongly recommend documenting agreements. Verbal agreements are convenient, but details can easily slip through the cracks. Who covers the shipping fees: artist or gallerist? How many hours do freelance staff commit to working each month? Was the agreed discount 5% or 50%? I'm not making these examples up; they are all drawn from past experiences. It's not about assuming bad intentions but about recognizing that details can be easily forgotten the day after they were discussed. Moreover, staff change and responsibilities shift. What might have been agreed verbally with one colleague may not be known by another. Don't overdo it. Sometimes, a simple WhatsApp message can be sufficient.

DOCUMENT AGREE-MENTS 24

25 DROP NAMES

Yes, you read it correctly: Drop names! But not in the way you might assume. The term usually refers to the technique of mentioning well-known and important people you know (or at least you know of, or your pet has traded sniffs with the pet of some celebrity's relative like how my dog once played with Armani's sister's dog. Impressive, right!?) to elevate your own position and status. However, what I am referring to is mentioning the names of your friends, allies, people with whom you have had a good experience in the past, people who are close to your heart, people who maybe need some support at a certain moment, to recommend their works or services to your network. Or in a more contemporary language, give them a shout-out. I do believe that this act will give you great satisfaction; and, on top of that and as I've said before, what goes around comes around. Positive vibes and recommendations will surely flow back to you.

26

MAKE ONE ROOM AS BEAUTI-FUL AS POS-SIBLE

“Try to make one room in your home as beautiful as possible” is the straightforward yet philosophical suggestion by Jordan B. Peterson in his book *Beyond Order*. He continues, “Making something beautiful is difficult, but it is amazingly worthwhile. We live by beauty. We live by literature. We live by art. Beauty can help us appreciate the wonder of Being.” Working in the art industry, we should try not to forget that, even though art becomes a commodity in many ways. Surround yourself with works that speak to you, with some design that gives you joy every day and functions as a reminder that art is not a luxury or affection but a necessity and pillar of our culture. With a little gracious self-promotion, @larrys_list gathers examples by amazing talents on how to bring art, design, and architecture together for those seeking some inspiration on just how to achieve this.

On a daily basis, many of us are bombarded with numerous inquiries. These requests often go beyond a simple response like "yes," "no," "Tuesday to Saturday," "nothing available," or "we can add you to our waiting list." They frequently require you to invest precious time to research, investigate, and properly formulate a comprehensive answer. Examples include questions such as: How much does it cost to ship an artwork from London to Rome? Can you provide an overview of prices from the last solo show? What's the appropriate diet for my balloon dog?
When faced with requests from unfamiliar senders, I suggest you first validate how serious this inquiry really is. Prefab some standard emails. Keep it nice and short and don't spend too much time on the first communication, as, unfortunately, many requests turn out to be not so serious or lack depth. Once you have received more information (or have even talked on the phone), you can respond in more detail. This approach will ultimately save you valuable time.

27

QUALIFY THE RE-QUEST

USE SWARM INTELLI-GENCE

28

Two sets of eyes are often better than one. There are occasions when seeking a second professional opinion becomes essential, especially from individuals we trust. This is the moment when our art world crew comes in. While I hold strong opinions myself and take responsibility for my decisions, there are many occasions when another pair of eyes and set of ears are needed: A trusted friend to discuss a new abstract artist's position, an ally well-versed in Chinese art to evaluate whether to recommend a certain work to a collector, an arty brain who helps to decode a curatorial statement. I do enjoy every second of conversation with them. In fact, often these discussions are one of the reasons I remain in the art world. Returning to the initial thought, it's important to note that I don't always follow their judgments; but the discussions themselves are undeniably helpful and often joyful, becoming a reliable source of happiness throughout it all.

THINK TWICE WITH ART START-UPS

29

At least once a month, we are approached by people proposing to invest, collaborate, or serve on the board of their latest art company. The "unique" startup ideas range from NFT sites (less so recently) to art community platforms, and "new concepts" on how to sell art. Don't misunderstand me, I will always be excited about new ideas and developments, and even find the concept of retiring on the status quo uncomfortable. But like other industries, there is a lot of hot air in the market.

Also, don't underestimate how conservative our beloved art scene is and might continue to be for the foreseeable future. The basic principles of the art market have not changed, even though many people want to make you believe differently, and there are only very few people in the arts who really make money including some brick-and-mortar businesses like some art shippers.

It is also interesting that these new concepts often originate from people outside the art world. The new art social media platforms are proposed by people who don't understand how unsocial the art worlds often is; this new company seeking to bring in transparency and tracing possibilities is conceived by purely tech guys; the "oh-so-radical" fractionalization model of art investment is being sold to us by those only with finance backgrounds. If we glued all the barcodes and RFID tags ever proposed to us on each canvas, surely the standard size of canvases would be much larger by now.

Don't believe me? Send me the name of a new art business founded in the past five years that has really taken off and become a major player in the market. Notably, not every startup has the ambition to make big money, which is a fair point. But if it is not a charity, the company still has to demonstrate there is demand for the new product or service, and that is mostly measured in business done. So I suggest you think twice if you want to invest your time and money into any "not-yet-seen" art startup.

The art world speaks another language, especially on social media. If you understand the underlying principle, which is mostly about flexing, you will find it easier to decode the terms and phrases employed. Here are some common examples:

30 KNOW HOW TO DECODE SOCIAL MEDIA POSTS

Caption:	Translation:
"I am extremely grateful to @xxxgallery for this amazing painting."	"Neener neener, I got something you did not!" (Note: Photography or video works are never mentioned, sculpture or installation rarely).
"Xxx series of works are my favorites … The colors, details, shapes, and textures here are just incredible."	"Look at me! I can easily list all the characteristics (including even colors. OMG!) of an artwork in a single sentence."
"Best of luck for the future …"	"To the artist, gallerist, and other collectors, but especially to myself: Fingers crossed that I can cash in some artworks soonest."
"Thanks for having me at the xxx gallery opening/artist yyy's studio/art fair zzz preview."	"I am at peak art social demand as a recognized collector/curator/artist. Don't you wish you could be as popular as me?"
"Wet canvas."	"A wet dream come true! I'll be making money quickly off the back of this young artist."

As you read this, the first reason that comes to your mind for avoiding VIP lounges is probably due to the lack of privacy. Yes, but this is only one of many reasons. By the time you sit down for the actual meeting, you will have overcome a number of obstacles that often feel like an IRL jump-and-run game. Swapping multiple times to get in the shortest queue for drinks (lounges are notorious for a combined lack of table service and overly relaxed service staff) before, during, and/or after hovering around to find two (don't even dream about three) seats close together. This leads to your meeting being delayed by 15 to 25 minutes, effectively cutting down the meeting time by half. Then once you are sitting down, you are constantly bumping shoulders with people who often don't want to be nice but rather want to show others how many people they know while loudly demonstrating that they, too, have a VIP pass. All things considered, the 7-Eleven café around the corner might just be a better meeting spot.

P.S. Let me also mention that during the meeting, out of courtesy, please do focus on your conversation partner, and don't be constantly looking around like you're hoping to find someone more important to speak to.

31

AVOID VIP LOUNGES FOR MEETINGS

32

RE-SPECT THE LO-CALITY

I am always amazed by the density of art societies, city art groups, museum friends, Kunsthallen, etc. located in Central Europe. These organizations have functioned for decades and even centuries, allowing people to come together and exchange about their passion, and also showcase members' own art creations at times. Unquestionably, some works shown are not masterpieces. That passion does not necessarily translate into talent must be accepted (btw, what is your take on sand art?). But this is not the matter. Let's not look arrogantly at artworks that might not align with our oh-so-professional-hailing-from-Zürich/Berlin/LA view. While the local creators should be respected, so should the local audience. For the in-town-only-when-it-is-opening-night curators who head these institutions, sometimes the locals seem like a decoration for the show rather than the intended audience. Don't forget to apply your concept of diversity here also, please.

Over the years, I have come across few journalists in our industry who have their own independent opinions and who are not biased. Of course, being an art writer is not easy: Invitations to posh dinners, exclusive previews, and interviews with superstar artists while at the same time receiving financial compensation often at the bottom of the art world. The media, and hence, the writers, can have their own agendas, incentives, or clients to serve. This is not always bad, but it should be taken into consideration when consuming media. That "artist hot pick" or "curator's choice" is possibly sponsored by some gallery or dealer either directly or indirectly. Maybe it is obvious to my readers, but I at least need a constant reminder that in a world with so many opinions and so much noise, we must critically reflect on the information, news, and articles we are offered and leave our naïveté at the door.

RE-FLECT ON THE MEDIA

33

34

DON'T LOVE ART FOR THE MONEY

Are you ready for this advice? Take out the monetary aspect of art as much as, and wherever, possible. A respected colleague said to me not long ago, "The world is very fragile, and art and the art market are no exception. We must be careful in the art world that we don't lose relevance." What would happen if we instrumentalized art exclusively for the investment aspect and focused purely on financial gains? You don't have to look far; that is exactly what we witnessed in 2021 and 2022 when the NFT market exploded. Case in point, artist Beeple would not have become a household name (at least for the art world) if his artwork had not fetched a record price. Money puts things on the map. This is not new. I will never forget how I was approached by a senior banker from UniCredit in a bar. When he heard that I was in the art business, he told me that he was going to quit his job soon and focus on NFTs. How do we look at the situation a few months (a few months, not even years!) later? NFTs that sold for millions are now worth close to nothing. It's not my intention to bash NFTs (maybe a bit) but we see what happens if artistic concepts, aesthetic values, and meaning are lacking. This applies not only for NFTs but to artworks in general: No value increase leads most often to no more interest. Let's hope that the banker did not quit his job in the end.

One of the main reasons why I experience unhappiness in the art world is due to my own disillusionment. I believe I have a rather good understanding of the art market and its basic principles: It is guided by supply and demand and the influence of branding; there is an intrinsic value of quality; exhibitions in well-known museums matter, as do academic training, grants, and stipends. Alongside are the less visible rules—the networks of market makers, gatekeepers, and collectors—, an area and dynamic in which I believe I also have good insight. However, is a mere understanding and application of those rules enough? Spoiler alert: It is absolutely not. Just like in the real world, fair play is not always part of the deal. A “better” artist is not necessarily the more significant, more expensive, and more successful artist. A vulgar headline often gains more attention than

DON’T COUNT

a sophisticated one. A loud and lurid exhibition can be more visited than a subtle and silent one. Dirty jogging pants can gain you entrance into the Olympus of arts; but aesthetic in appearance, speech, and behavior maybe not. Perhaps you don't belong to the right family or were born without the right connections. The collectors that make the top lists speak so loudly, walking with legs spread like they just finished the longest rodeo, but only acquired a work on paper for which they demanded a 30% discount. The list goes on.

That does not stop me from continuing to advocate for logic, common sense, expertise, and good behavior. But I am also aware that this is not a guarantee of success. In a positive light, we could argue that the art world is always full of surprises, and happiness comes from the acceptance that some things can't be explained and don't make sense: They are the way they are, and probably that's ok.

35 ON RULES

36 STICK BUMPER STICK-ERS

The best things are often the simplest and should give you a smile every day. So, I am sharing here some of my favorite quotes and memes. Use them. Print them out. Stick them on your car, your laptop, or your shipping crate.

- Stay horny for art

- Honk if you like group shows!

- Please be yourself.
  This is not an art gallery.

- I wish I could invoice people for wasting my time.

- "Damn bro, your flat is all fucking IKEA." "I know.
  I spent all the money I had for furniture on art."

- My prices are based on my talent, not on your budget.

Since the launch of the first booklet, we have witnessed a rise in art scamming. I am not talking about the usual spam emails like "I got this Monet painting from my distant uncle who recently passed away. A famous scholar has valued the work at Euro 35 million, but if you pay now, it can be yours for Euro 19.999 including shipping." Scams are now much more sophisticated, becoming harder to spot due to identity theft and phishing. Examples we've seen include invoices seemingly sent from the gallery you have agreed to buy works from with just a few small differences like "Ltd" in the company name or sent from a .co email address instead of .com, and, of course, with a different bank account number. A friend even told me that the art gangsters knew that they were away on holiday and offered them payment after their return, ending the email with "Say hello to the dog." Even more common are fake social media accounts purporting to be well-known art-world figures that ask for upfront payment for curatorial services and such alike. In a recent article, Simon de Pury complained that such fraud had occurred to him when the fraudsters used a variation of his Instagram handle.

My advice: No shipping of works before payment, no money transfer before checking it is legit, and always double-check account information via two independent communication channels. With the ever-advancing development of deep fake image and voice technologies, expect things to become even more "exciting" in the near future.

37 BE CAUTIOUS OF SIMONE DEL PURY

Cold red wine out of (reusable) plastic cups, no canapés, no fancy business address (not because of a marketing stunt but because that's all they can afford), a gallerist that picks up artworks from the artist in an old van and delivers right to the show: I like small businesses. The purchase of an artwork or giving them a project can really make a change for them. So even if you have heard this from me before, I can't emphasize it enough: Let's support them!

SUP-PORT SMALL BUSINESS-ES 38

DON'T BE SE-DUCED BY THE VIP LA-BEL

39

Art fair VIP lounges that look like a tier-three city airport offering snacks (no matter complimentary or overpriced) that resemble Deutsche Bahn train bistro quality and selection, exclusive previews where you have to queue to get inside, private events that are more packed than a Primark discount sale, Biennale media days that are so crowded that after 20 minutes of waiting you realize you did not queue for the most-discussed art installation but for the Campari bar (maybe good for you actually). “VIP,” “exclusive,” “private,” etc. are words that are used broadly in the art world. Therefore, I propose to select your presence carefully and less according to the terminology.

The art market, as any market, follows the principles of supply and demand. To a large extent, this defines the price of an artwork. I don't want to delve into all the criteria that contribute to setting the price, like quality, medium, size, biography of the artist, etc., but rather to look at it from another side: from the perspective of the gallery that sells the work. A huge space in London's Mayfair, business class trips for gallery staff to Miami, hotel rooms during peak season, fancy client entertainment, prestigious external PR specialists, sales directors that only drink Voss water (maybe also bathe in it?), legal departments, and more all create huge overhead costs that must be covered somehow (and, more precisely, by someone). So, if you sometimes wonder why mediocre artworks are so expensive, try factoring in all those expenses. If you think about it, you won't be confused by the quality-to-price logic anymore.

40

UNDER-STAND HOW PRIC-ES ARE CALCULAT-ED

41 PLAY ART BULL-SHIT BINGO

Because laughing is important. The rules are simple: Whoever says the word/expression during a conversation checks the box. The first person to check all boxes loses and must put USD 5/Euro 5/one NFT into the prize pool. The first person to win five rounds takes all.

P.S. We still need platitudes. Without them, this booklet probably wouldn't exist.

great potential	hot artist	defies classifica-tion	I am so tired of art fairs
reject binary thinking	at the intersection	Are you doing Basil?	juxta-posing
let's catch up soon	post-colonialism	so jetlagged	transdisci-plinary
underesti-mated	Can you get me a VIP pass?	overpriced	We are Insta friends

MASTER CON- TENT

42

OVER MAR- KETING

Nowadays, it seems like marketing is more and more overshadowing the actual product or service it is meant to be promoting. This happens in fashion, luxury, and music; and art is no exception. "On the runway, red carpet and beyond, culture is at risk of being subsumed by the sound and the fury, the hype and the buzz, of its own promotion," shares Natasha Degen in her recent opinion for *The New York Times*. We see fashion directors hired less for their design skills and more for their marketing power. In the art world, artists are added to the gallery roster for their large presence on social media rather than the quality of their works. While marketing and promotion are nothing new, it used to start with the product (aka art) and then the promotion was built around it. Now, the noise often overwhelms the actual content, the piece, the craft, the intended meaning of the art. Think about the HD clips advertising exhibition previews or the hype about queueing to see a work or, better, to take a selfie with it. Let us be conscious that we do not make art itself irrelevant in the end. Creating relevant (and maybe also less) content might be a first step to doing so.

Yes, yes, the sky is the limit, and there are multiple occasions where I encourage my dear readers to follow their dreams, to go big, to bring new exciting things into creation, and to take a risk. I don't believe it is conflicting to say that at the same time you should be aware of your limits, and no matter how positively you think, a dose of realism can be extremely healthy. Working with famous clients does not make you famous. Working with rich collectors does not make you automatically rich. Just because you tasted a billionaire's lifestyle, be cautious that you are not trapped in a downward spiral that targets your whole existence to live at that same level, sacrificing integrity and reputation. People ending up at Alcatraz Island rather than Mykonos Island has happened before.

43

KNOW YOUR LIMITS

ENJOY UGLY

GREAT

Sounds like a luxury problem, hanging your Euro 25k painting over a bought-in-a-flash-sale, poor quality couch. We have had the pleasure of seeing many interiors of collectors, being invited into their most private spaces. Then, at the end of the apartment tour comes the question about our opinion of the interior design and the art. I try to avoid these conversations. Taste and style are arguably very personal, and multiple times we have witnessed art in indelicate interiors. Of course, there are the amazing, Instagram-worthy, Julie Hillman-styled interiors featuring magnificent art and design. But there is also often the lack of any sensitive, aesthetic appreciation for the surroundings of the artworks, including furniture, colors, textures, and so on.

44 ART IN INTERI-ORS

Quick hack if someone is asking: Use Farrow & Ball colors! No matter which of their color tones you choose, you can't go wrong. There can be an overall more exciting sensation of a mediocre artwork on a Farrow & Ball-painted wall than an expensive work in an unthought drab setting. I will face criticism for saying it, but sell one of your Euro x-amount paintings if you need cash and give the job to an interior designer to create your living space. I see design and interior architecture as equally important in the cultural equation … and in your living room. (And yes, great art in great interiors is top, but then again, not all can always be achieved at once.)

ACCEPT NOT TO MAKE MONEY 45

Some areas of the art industry will never allow you to make a decent living. Not today and not tomorrow. With a job as a junior gallery staff, even with (in some cases, especially with) a reputable name on your business card, you may not be able to survive in a major art hub unless you have additional income streams. Setting up your own gallery can be a long-desired dream and worth eating instant noodles for months, but happiness and a satisfied life originate from multiple factors. I am bringing this issue up because a lot of conversations with people who work in the art industry circle around how to make a living. The art scene is a strange mix of tremendous wealth alongside those just trying to get by. Why is money important? Because, more than allowing you to lead the life you want, it gives you the freedom to walk away from people and work you don't like.

Pressure on. From a new artwork drop that is only available for 24 hours (change to seconds if you prefer) to the gallery that asks you to send .jpgs of paintings before they are even painted for the next auction catalogue, we deal with deadlines on a daily basis. While they are a reality and agreements on timelines are a basic principle for harmonious coexistence, I suggest you critically ask if it is *really* a deadline or just a *suggestion*. A deadline often exercises power over others, and I have too often seen situations where they are used by superiors to manage subordinates.

46 CALL THE DEADLINE BLUFF

47

GET YOUR CHILD-REN SOME PROPER ART EDU-CATION

Art world parents listen again: This is a long shot for happiness. Unfortunately, many schools don't offer enough of the right type of art education. Surely, it can be already credited if the kids know that the *Last Supper* is not the opposite of a Happy Meal. While art history is certainly a valuable subject, art education should also strongly focus on encouraging thinking in creative ways. We still see that the best grades are often achieved when copying something directly. But an elephant could have wings. Or wear a wig. I don't see creative practice being encouraged enough. As we learned in #18, creative jobs will not die out any time soon. So, if your school does not provide this crucial skill, ensure your kid participates in an extracurricular activity that nurtures their creativity.

Over the past 15 years, I have collected thousands of business cards, contacts, and LinkedIn connections. I recently spent hours going through them one by one only to find that 95% of them are now useless. Most people have changed their original position, companies no longer exist, and email addresses have become invalid.
How many hours have I spent on networking activities, attending talks, scrolling social networks, and initiating conversations to compile this contact list? Obviously, this is not all wasted time, but in the end, how many people really matter? I would assume 50 at most. That makes it clear that we should carefully balance between quantity and quality. Bonding intensively with a few people and nourishing those relationships should always be a priority. I like to chat and have random conversations, and occasionally some ideas develop out of it. However, this strategy keeps you busy, taking time away from things that might be more fruitful.

Bonus hack on the topic of freeing up some time: Cancel meetings! If people were less stuck in meetings, they would have more time to get things done.

48 NOURISH QUALI-TY OVER QUANTI-TY

TRUST YOUR CURRENCY

49

This has been discussed on a number of occasions previously: The art scene is characterized by relationships, connections, and (less visible) networks. What is the currency of these relationships? Trust. It's something that takes long to build and seconds to lose. Remember that.

Regularly, I am confronted with this invisible group that forms opaque frameworks dictating much of what art is or is not acceptable. Not a small number of people, including artists and also a wider group of art lovers, are intimidated by this group of opinion makers and take their words for granted on topics such as which artist we are "allowed" to like, what art has any worth, who is hot or not, and which show or gallery can enforce or destroy an artist's career. This group is often formed by curators, writers, collectors (aka investors), gallerist in art fair selection committees, etc. trying to demonstrate their power and legitimacy. Surely, there are those with lots of knowledge, expertise, experience, and good intentions; but there are also those with politically, commercially, or personally motivated agendas.

A dear artist friend recently asked for my opinion on a project of designing a box for a traditional panettone bakery. He thought this commercial project might not be accepted by some curators. My advice: Do it if you think it is worth doing, and if it feels right for you. Let thousands of people enjoy your original and witty creations. Unhappiness happens because people try to fit into frameworks. Don't subordinate your opinion too much to those of others. You can't always change the framework, but you can decide if you want to operate in it or not.

50

CHAL-LENGE

FRAME-WORKS

51 DON'T RUIN THE EU-PHORIA OF OTHERS

It can be flattering and exciting, the feeling of being an experienced teacher explaining to newbies (and the not-so-new alike) how the art world functions. Often, I find myself in this role, and perhaps too often, my perspective highlights the problems rather than the opportunities as I take a moment to enjoy moaning about our "terrible" art scene. It can be tempting, for example, when someone euphorically shares their idea of opening a gallery, etc., to mentally, and also verbally, pull out a list of hundreds of reasons why this is an awful idea.

This appeal is to everyone, including my dear friends who feel that they are key players in the scene: Now it's your time to use your influence in a beneficial way. Your (positive) message is powerful! As discussed previously, do not underestimate how much a small sharing can influence others. The art world is based not only on facts but also on how we feel, think, and communicate about it. Key phrase: Self-fulfilling prophecy. So next time, encourage others who are making a positive contribution to our scene instead of brushing all positive intentions aside.

52 DON'T BE AN ART-HOLE

An arthole is a mix between an art person and … you know the rest. I'm not sure who came up with the expression, but the name is apt for more than a few. Here comes the challenge: Once you are dead, you don't know it; only others do. The same logic applies to being an arthole. No matter how rich, educated, or cool you are, what matters is how you treat other people. I am not impressed if you call your boss by their first name; it matters if you greet the cleaning lady. So, what is the advice here? There are many artholes around us, especially the longer you stay in the scene. If you are not one of them, you can be proud of yourself. Stay humble, because we have seen people become what they once laughed at.

Of course, much of the other advice directly or indirectly contributes to making the art world a happier place, but let's mention it here explicitly. The world seems like it is in a permanent state of crisis with things getting worse by the minute. However, when we start seeking out the positive, things are possibly getting better. Make it a rule to surround yourself with positive people and positive experiences, and the (art) world will become a positive place.

53 MAKE THE ART WORLD A POSITIVE PLACE

54 DON'T BURDEN YOURSELF

Several artists I have met show a high sensitivity towards the happenings around them and in the world in general. They try to make strong statements with their art, using their work to initiate discussions and call for action. Small steps are needed, and artists have a role. In parallel, we witness ultra-wealthy collectors looking closely at such artistic proposals. It is awkward that these people—the ones with the financial, political, and economic power to create change—are often passively watching, not taking the lead, and leaving the job and responsibility to the arts. This, then, is not a call to stop advocating for change through art, but a reminder that artists do not have to carry the weight of the world on their shoulders. (And still remember the environment next time you bubble wrap your work.)

We live in an age in which people ignore each other in order to get attention. This is partly the negative side of social media dynamics, where people focus more on projecting their own imagery rather than engaging meaningfully with others. Additionally, we see many people investing a lot of energy to get the attention of people who are not looking. Confusing times. To overcome this, I suggest developing your personal micro audiences. Micro sounds small, but not necessarily. Here is where social media comes in handy: A niche can be huge because you can reach a global audience interested in your doings with a simple well-placed hashtag.

55 DE-VELOP MICRO AU-DIENCES

56

APPRECIATE THE PERSON, NOT THE TITLE

Have we not all experienced when a person flashes a fancy business card with a top art gallery or auction house name (or automotive brand, fashion label, etc.), only to let the brand and their position leave a more memorable impression than their own personality? (That a company needs exactly this type of employee is a different topic in itself.) I have always been more impressed by the person rather than by the title. Based on that, I have come to two conclusions: Firstly, don't hide your personality behind a role, becoming just a "gallery girl" or an auction house staff. Secondly, when doing business, consider going with the right person and not the flashy art brand or hot gallery. For example, as an artist, the director of a humbler gallery who impressed you with their keen insight into your message might be more of a pleasure to work with; and as a collector, perhaps a smaller gallery with staff that remember your face and not just your credit card details might give you better customer service.

WISH TO NEVER LOSE THE ABILITY TO SEE HOW BEAUTIFUL ART CAN BE

57

Nothing to add.

One of the things I enjoy doing the most is having a casual dinner with art friends and colleagues. Typically a mix of a bit private and a bit professional, with good food and drinks to stimulate creative thinking; not seldom new projects have developed out of such conversations. On a side note: I think that a Chinese dinner where everyone shares dishes can be warmer than a German-style dinner where everyone looks only at their own plate with a Schnitzel for 20 minutes. If you think that a dinner might be too much of a commitment, the Italians have invented something beautiful: the aperitivo. Aperitivo is timed between coffee and dinner, around 5 to 7 pm, meaning it is not a catch-up over coffee or as committed as a dinner. If the aperitivo is enjoyable, you can always extend it into a spontaneous dinner.

GO FOR A HAPPY MEAL (OR AN APERITIVO)

58

Some argue that nothing is truly original, and new ideas are often derived from existing ones, blending and remixing them. However, this doesn't justify the obvious, unscrupulous, and unethical copying we frequently see in artistic imagery, writings, social media presentations, and more. While inspiration is essential, it is crucial to give credit where credit is due. How can seeing your work reinterpreted with just a few minor edits and no mention of your name lead to happiness? It's a small yet significant joy to know that you are the original creator and are at least being secretly admired for it.

On a final note, don't forget that sometimes what seems to be a clearcut case of "stolen inspiration" is not so. Ideas can develop simultaneously in different areas and parts of the world. Then it becomes about who can better execute the idea in the long run.

59

COME TO PEACE WITH COPY-CATS

FUCK ALL ART AD-VICE BOOKS

60

People will tell you there are many secrets in the art world. What they really want is to make you believe they are smarter than you. So, forget about all the advice books. Here is everything you need to know (and probably already knew anyway):

For collectors:
1. Buy what you like.
2. Most art does not appreciate in value.
3. Water, sunlight, and sticky Nutella children's fingers don't harmonize well with artworks (no matter which medium).

For artists:
1. It is hard to sustain a career by selling artworks; it is even harder to sustain a career by not selling them.

For everyone else:
1. If you need guidance on how to distinguish between good and bad art, sorry; only time will tell.
2. Most art does not appreciate in value.
3. If you enjoy your time in the art world, stay. If not, do something else.

That's it. The rest is pretentious blah blah.

IM-
PRINT

Editor: Christoph Noe
Editing: Jamie Bennett

Supported by: Jamie Bennett, Arianna Ambrosetti, Cordelia Noe, Summer Tsui, George Frederick Takis
Produced by: LARRY'S LIST

Design: Raphael Drechsel

Published by:
VfmK Verlag für moderne Kunst GmbH
Schwedenplatz 2/24
1010 Vienna, Austria
www.vfmk.org

ISBN 978-3-99153-134-0

Printed in Czech Republic

Distribution:

Europe: LKG, www.lkg-va.de

UK: Cornerhouse Publications, www.cornerhouse-publications.org

USA: D.A.P., www.artbook.com

Bibliographic information published by the Deutsche Nationalbibliothek

The Deutsche Nationalbibliothek lists this publication in the Deutsche Nationalbibliografie; detailed bibliographic data is available in the Internet at dnb.de